Contents

Mouse Maze

Mouse went out.

Mouse went over.

Mouse went up.

Mouse went in.

3

Mouse went along.

Mouse went under.

Mouse went down.

Mouse went home.

4

5

Hop, Skip, Jump

Written by Luther Roiata ► Illustrated by Hui-Yao Hsu

box

ladder

pole

squares

ne

Start here

tunnel

Hop along the squares.
Hop, hop, hop.

Jump over the box.
Jump, *jump,* jump.

Climb up the ladder.

Climb, climb, climb.

Slide down the pole.
Slide, slide, slide.

Crawl under the net.
Crawl, crawl, crawl.

Run into the tunnel.
Run, run, run.

Go back home.
Hop, skip, *jump*.

15

Monster Moves

Written by Avelyn Davidson

Illustrated by Sandra Camme

Come on.
Come and hop.
Come and hop
like a frog.

17

Come on.
Come and crawl.
Come and crawl
like a caterpillar.

19

Come on.
Come and slide.
Come and slide
like a snake.

21

On the Move

I leap.

I waddle.

I crawl.

I slither.

Make a Mobile

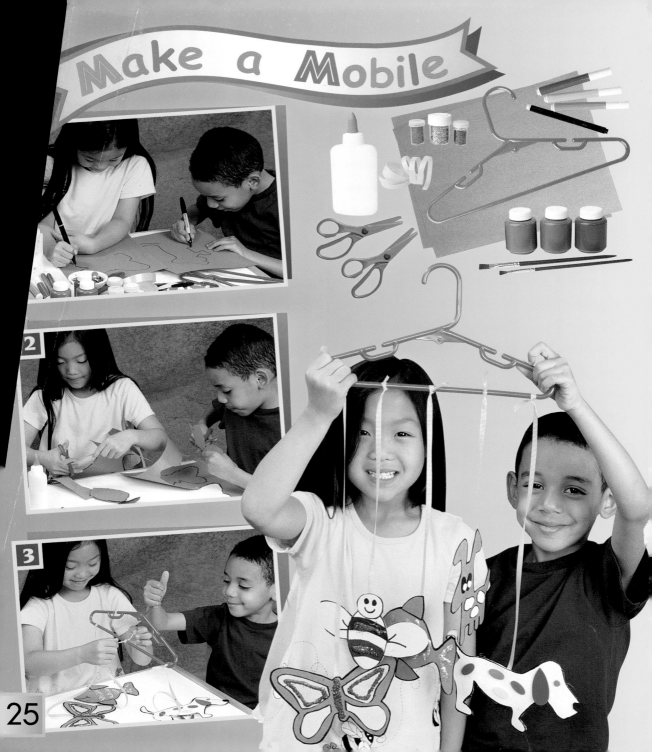

Messy Mons

We crawl into the tunnel.

We hide inside.

31

We run on the bridge.

We climb on the frame.

Come and play
our keep fit game!

We Like to Jog

We like to jog.

We like to jog by a log.

34

Come and play
our keep fit game!

We Like to Jog

We like to jog.

We like to jog by a log.

34

Our Keep Fit Game

Written by
Elizabeth Pulford

Illustrated by
Jennifer Coon

We swing on the swings.

We slide on the slide.

I fly.

I run.

I jump.

I swim.

I slide.

27

Find the
odd one out.

28

You mustn't mention monsters
to my mother.
Monsters make my mother
moan and roar.
Some messy monsters
came to play last Monday,
and made messy marks
all over Mother's floor!

Look!

A frog by the log.

The log likes to jog.

Letters I Know

 Mm

Sounds I Know

 -og

Words I Know

a	come	in	over	up
along	down	like	the	we
and	I	on	under	went